This book is dedicated to my loved ones
who watched me fade away mentally,
nursed me back to health and showed me
that love lives from within.
Thank you for all being there in times of
need.
This book is for anyone suffering or has
suffered domestic abuse. It is for the
women before and after me.
A ode to all women.
It is a collection of my poetry.
The last few pages are reminders that
you will get through the abuse.
I pray you heal.

If I stripped myself of the clothes
the world has put on my back and
started again,
maybe then you'd see my womanhood.
 Maybe then you'd understand
a woman's pain,
how she drowns in mysogony to survive.
How dare you
take the anatomy of women and
 brand it 'imperfect'
how dare you
decide it is offensive and should be hidden.
How dare you tell us what to wear and how
dare you decide the fates of women after
me that deserve to be liberated.
How dare you tell us who we are.
How dare you abuse us
I will not be silenced.
We will not drown in despair.
 I refuse to water down what happened to
me and so many other women.

A.Thorne-Miles

You manipulated me into believing love was all I had
How many other women will be spun in your web? How many women did I fail by not speaking up
The thoughts of my guilty conscience

A.Thorne-Miles

I swore to myself,
I would take every bad part
of each person that broke my heart,
and blame it on you.
Why else would you have sent them?
The ill thoughts of my mind.

A.Thorne-Miles

Loving you is like an ocean wave;
I can't breathe your grip is so tight.

A. Thorne-Miles

We borrowed souls
 never with the intention to buy.
Love is freedom.
Why is it I still know the date of your
receipt.
All we did was borrow souls.

A.Thorne-Miles

When people ask if I believe in
soul mates
I tell them no
It pains me to know I drowned
you with my despair.
I thought feelings were to be
shared.

A.Thorne-Miles

I spend most mornings showering in your
abuse
It leaves scrapes on the surface.
It will never clean out the past abuse
that lives underneath.
I suppose that made you the one for me.

A.Thorne-Miles

You chewed me whole
then spat me out
You were left standing,
in a puddle of broken memories;
I guess we are made up of mostly water.

A.Thorne-Miles

The lies you sold to me left me
walking on ice,
They were so thin they cut my feet.

A.Thorne-Miles

I loved you more than myself,
In the end
all you gave back were words,
Words so vile,
you'd be drunk from swallowing
them.

A.Thorne-Miles

Your eyes were deeper than
oceans
So filled with meaning,
hope and prosperity
Why did you let the world
pollute them?

A.Thorne-Miles

Your mouth turned the rain acidic.

A. Thorne-Miles.

You flooded my mind with your vindictive
words
I purge in the mornings out of fear,
 fear,
  you are watching?
Somebody turn the cameras off
 I would beg.
Please stop the recordings playing back.
 I couldn't take it anymore,
 I would plead. Little did I know I was
having flashbacks, a product of
psychosis.
 That you caused.

A.Thorne-Miles

Kissing you was like drinking poison
 that tasted like lemon and honey.
I couldn't get enough until my tongue
turned bitter.

A.Thorne-Miles

Our love was temporary.
You washed me away as if
 I were a pebble under your foot,
with that; I decided to swim.

A. Thorne-Miles

You seduced me with your love for
planet earth.
Why wasn't I a part of her?
You gave me the soil
 I painted the sky.
It was never enough.

A.Thorne-Miles

You were like a god to me.
Your weeping whispered gold
Your love was forever cold and
conditional
You made me question existence?

A.Thorne-Miles

I can still see the reflection of your face in my tears.

A.Thorne-Miles

I hope
you
drown
in the blood
from my broken heart.

A.Thorne-Miles

If I rinsed your touch off of
my skin
  would it rain with knives?
Would it slice my lungs open?
Maybe, that's why I still can't
breathe.

A.Thorne-Miles

Sometimes I feel like I'm washing in dirty water. I'm surrounded by the abuse.
It clings onto my skin so tightly it begins to suffocate me

A. Thorne-Miles

You never gave me the chance to float
 above your waterfall of an ego.
I learnt to swim alone.

A.Thorne-Miles

I swallowed your venom whole;
does that make me a whore?
Even washing it out with holy water
 wouldn't make me feel loved.

A.Thorne-Miles

I would bow down to my knees in
devotion, begging to be loved.
You had no respect for my female
anatomy.
Was I not good enough?

A.Thorne-Miles

I would have done anything to wash
my impure skin
 in your predilection for pretty
and pure girls.
Just to taste what it felt like to
be beautiful in your eyes, instead
of her.

A.Thorne-Miles

You smashed the bones in my soul
one by one
Then scattered the ashes
 knowing you'd already killed me.

A.Thorne-Miles

If there is one thing I learned from you it's,
  how not to die drowning on disrespect.

A.Thorne-Miles

I would wash my skin with razor blades,
just to feel alive again.
The soul that you destoryed.

A.Thorne-Miles

I would bath in boiling hot water
just to feel the burn on my skin,
I wanted to be pure for you.
I slowly realised, I was killing myself.

A.Thorne-Miles

You would hold me in your arms
  then let me go,
  push me away.
Make me feel dirty.
The bruises I gathered like gifts
They made me feel clean.
How can I support other women
  when I still love you?
You made me feel worthless
  to my own kind.

A.Thorne-Miles

You would demand I fed you,
then not turn up for your
food.
My Mother always said
' don't bite the hand that feeds
you.'
 It was then I realised that
I pick the skin on my fingers
because
 that's all the men in my life had
ever done.

A.Thorne-Miles

My bruises aren't all metophorical.
 I could list all of the things you did,
I just can't bring myself to risk my life.

I did not survive a bruised heart
 to have it ripped out of my once
 fragile chest.
I did not heal from interanl and
external bruises
for my heart to stop beating
at your hands.

A.Thorne-Miles

I was baptised in the sea to wash
myself of the sins
you subdued me to.

A.Thorne-Miles

You froze me
left me to melt with the dirt seeping
out.
It felt like guilt rained on me.
I've never felt so dirty.

A.Thorne-Miles

I was completely love blind
I forgave you time and time again
but you see my love
I saw the fear in you
took advantage
Walked away
So I could live to see another day

A.Thorne-Miles

I was hospitalised so many times from the mental abuse, I began to think I deserved it

A.Thorne-Miles

I believed you could do anything
If you told me you could walk on water,
 I would have believed you.
I saw you the same as I saw my father;
you were invincible to me.

A.Thorne-Miles

I could spit hatred at you for the rest of
my life,
Drink your blood like it's water
You took my sanity with you,
  for that I can never forgive you.

A.Thorne-Miles

I wish we could wash away our mistakes,
start over.
You broke me.
I just couldn't afford to look back.
Everything I did was never enough.

A.Thorne-Miles

I don't know why I still love you.
Every tear I shed,
I remember how pathetic you made me
feel.
I will never be sorry for your
misogynistic beliefs.

A.Thorne-Miles

You never could quite get me to
boiling point.
Maybe then I'd have been pure
enough.

A.Thorne-Miles

I slapped myself in the face repeatedly.
 Screaming for forgiveness.
Your forgiveness.
I smashed my head against the bath
until I could barely see.
I just wanted to feel you one last time
before I knew I had to say goodbye.

A.Thorne-Miles

I drank other poisons and still yours
was the only one to slide so smoothly
down my throat.

I just can't let you go.

A.Thorne-Miles

My father always said
"be careful of pulling those faces, if the
wind changes you'll stay like that".
Since our hurricane of love ended,
I haven't smiled since.

A.Thorne-Miles

I still try to heal myself every day,
but somehow slowly a splash of
your iniquity still falls onto my eyelash
leaving me wondering why
 I didn't listen to my father
when he said you were no good.
Somehow I still manage to feel like he was
wrong.
A domestic abuse victim at it's finest.

A.Thorne-Miles

Some days I wake up and
 miss the taste of your foolishness,
it almost seemed,
looking back that you
never meant for it to be so abusive.
Illicit lustre might have been the cause
something I will always ponder.
Or am I just nowhere near
truly recovered?

A. Thorne-Miles

I have never loved somebody
 the way I loved you
completely unconditional

the way you smiled
the way you laughed
I know you're never going to read this,
but, you're the one that got away
how selfish was I
to save you for a rainy day

the rainy day came
and you never came home,
 I guess I have to say that
I'm forever alone.

~I am still recovering from
 narcissistic abuse

A.Thorne-Miles

I withdraw from your hands on my head,
stroking it like silk,
  then I remember that same head you took
and smashed against a boiler.

I hold my head on bad days
in fear of the people behind me,
I trust nobody.
Not even myself.

I rocked back and forth,
holding my head for 3 hours thinking
I was going to die.

You will never have been my insomniacs
lullaby.

A.Thorne-Miles

They say what you do comes back to you
  three times.
I deserved what you did to me.
But no other woman does, no man does.

Why do I think I deserved it
if I would never believe that
  for another human being?

You taught me how to
drown myself in hate.
You taught me
what not loving yourself looks like.
that is why
  I hardly ever write anything happy

A.Thorne-Miles

I am sorry that you projected
your trauma onto me.

.

A.Thorne-Miles

Somebody once told me
if you don't look at
the love you have around you,
you'll look for it in all the wrong places.
I learned I am love.
You are love.
Going our separate ways
was the best thing we could have done.
I pray that love rains on me
from within
and drenches me with
the ability to be whole again.
Despite everything
 I pray you can be whole again.

A.Thorne-Miles

I slipped out of my family's fingers
and my sanity along with it.

A.Thorne-Miles

I still mourn the day I met you.

A.Thorne-Miles

The sanity you took
as if it were a trinket
to be kept with pride
 will forever remain
by your side because
that girl you abused
 doesn't exist anymore.
She is damaged,
 but the courage she holds
could wash you away
with her words of love.
Kill him with kindness she whispered.

A.Thorne-Miles

I resented my mother for calling you
 'scum of the earth'
In reflection
we are all born from the earth.
It helped me to forgive you: you bring
flames to burn it down,
 but you've spent your life
trying to fix it
 through watering the plants
 you'd abandoned.

A.Thorne-Miles

I've never been addicted
to anything more
than the way you treated me
at first.
I shouldn't have trusted you.

A.Thorne-Miles

Thank you for helping me to swim
in my own insanity.
It made me who I am today.

A.Thorne-Miles

You blinded me with your love.
I had sleep paralysis.
You threw acid in my eyes.
I awoke and my face
was wet with sweat.
The broken mind I was left with.

A.Thorne-Miles

The loss of sanity I experienced
 was something that would
make me want to
spend an eternity in hell
than to ever lose my mind again like that.
I spent months in hospital deluded;
you destroyed me.
Temporarily.

A.Thorne-Miles

I cried so many tears, I can no longer cry.
I'm filled to the brim with tablets to
stabilize my mind.
The mind you stepped on like a child to a
muddy puddle.

A.Thorne-Miles

I asked myself every morning
  when I would heal
from the organ you played
so melodically and
then smashed
because
it didn't play a tune
you liked anymore,
Like a child
throwing toys
out of their pram;
you had the audacity
  to call me the baby.

A.Thorne-Miles

You filled your challace with
unholiness,
 filled with demonic water and
drank from it knowing
I'd spend the rest of my life in fear.

A.Thorne-Miles

I chose to love somebody
over blood; I'll never forgive myself.

A.Thorne-Miles

You gave me drugs for my birthday,
 I swallowed them with water
wanting to feel courage men
 before you had diminished.
 I don't blame you for my addictions.
 I blame you for showing me that
nobody truly cares
whether you live or die.

A.Thorne-Miles

My life was disposable to you,
it seems all life is,
apart from the plants you grow to
consume for yourself.
 I should rename you 'the soul sucker.'
You took energy I didn't have and nearly
left me to die.

A.Thorne-Miles

I opened up to you about wanting to commit
suicide:
fading, wanting to die, wanting peace.
You pushed me in the chest
and the oceans kissed my eyes.
Nobody ever made me feel so alone.
I will never understand
why you did these things to me.

A.Thorne-Miles

There are so many things I want to say,
but
It's never going to be ok
to write that down,
all the things you did to me.
I could never put somebody through
having to read that.
Still you silence me from afar.
I tremble at the thought of you
ever reading this or any of my work.

A.Thorne-Miles

I dreamt of you
cutting my stomach open and
calling me a whore.
 I guess a result of the multiple stab
threats I received after
I finally broke away.
I rinsed them out of my heart.
My mind will never be the same.

A.Thorne-Miles

I can never excuse your actions.
This book is my healing process.
I still believe we're soul mates;
a product of
obsessive compulsive disorder.
I obsess over thinking of you
in a way
any domestic violence worker
would have me sectioned
all over again for.

A Thorne-Miles

Our love was a well;
every time
somebody dropped a coin in it,
overspilling was the result.

A.Thorne-Miles

I resent you for a lot of things,
but what I don't is holding me
 when my pipes would burst
with hot water burning your skin.
I'm sorry
for all the vile words
I was drunk swallowing.
More paradoxical forgiveness.
Dellusional love.

A.Thorne-Miles

I found art in my scars,
you found vengeance in yours.

A.Thorne-Miles

I thought I deserved it.
It was you
who deserved to drown
in your own guilt,
if you even have any.

A.Thorne-Miles

you destroyed me.
But i'm not going to give
you that power,
I will overcome this.
I will be stronger,
strength is something my
parents gave to me innately
You will never reach the
water on the top of my
mountain;
 I saved that for myself in
times of thirst when I need
it.
That's how I'm still alive.

A.Thorne-Miles

I saw you through eyes
incomprehensible;
you were perfect to me.

A. Thorne-Miles

Like water to wine;
miracles you performed
 before my eyes.
In the end
they were manipulation tactics
to fill the fish tank with water
that was my mind at the time.
I could never remember what you had said
when we argued, almost like a three second
memory.
 I guess that's how your magic tricks went
on for so long.

A. Thorne-Miles

For my roses sipping on rain
in a world where the sun does
not shine.

You should never beg to be loved,
or beg someone to stay with you.
If they do not want to be with you,
 walk away.
Let the tsunami behind your eyes pour
The 'one' would never leave you
or have you beg for love.
Go and find yourself and love will find you.

A. Thorne-Miles

I ask myself some days If I'm healed and
sometimes the answer is no.
But that is okay my dear
because before the sun rises,
the sky must first
be filled with darkness.

A.Thorne-Miles

Healing is the hardest part of the process.
 I meditated,
prayed and fasted,
I was even baptised in the sea,
I learnt to speak in tongues.
I was praying he would come back to me
changed.
In the end it was still my fault.
I know now it wasn't.
I just can't help but still blame myself
for losing what we had.
 I have days where I cry for him and
 days where I tremble at the idea
of facing him again.

A.Thorne-Miles

Healing is a process
. A long one,
it takes an entire lifetime.
You are worth a lifetime.

A. Thorne-Miles

It will one day get better.
You are strong and brave,
you deserve a love that lasts.
The kind of love you always dreamt of.
 A love that leaves you
tingling with warmth
,a love that leaves you breathless
because you have never seen
anything so beautiful

A.Thorne-Miles

You are love.
A reminder for some
of what we are
in the eyes of our mothers,
for some a reminder
of our reflection.
If we weren't love ,
how is it
we are so capable of loving another?

A.Thorne-Miles

We are all so beautiful. Handmade
creations.
 Guard your heart,
never let it shatter
 at the strikes of someone so cruel.
You hold the power to move mountains,
you just have to believe.

A.Thorne-Miles

You are strong and courageous.
Your eyes are filled
 with the earth
and your feet, I promise you
are truly flat on the ground.
No matter how much you feel
like you're levitating above water
 about to drown
the minute you're dropped.
Your feet are firmly on the ground.

A.Thorne-Miles

A domestic violence worker
once told me 'some things
you'll just never get over'
 I now don't take this as true.
 I stopped sleeping with a knife
under my pillow and
I stopped checking the window
to see if he was still following me.
People want to help and
they can help.
You just have to start by calling that
number you've been afraid to call.
You are love.
Love doesn't deserve
to not be loved.

A.Thorne-Miles

Leave them behind, it's not your fault.
 If I had a 'wishing well'
that I could Fill with the tears of
 abused men and women,
the world would shudder.

A.Thorne-Miles

Abuse comes in many forms
this book is one of them;
I have abused myself for writing of
forgiveness to a person who took my
temple and abused it.
You will do the same,
 make excuses and find forgiveness
but in the end,
 they truly do deserve
to drown in their guilt.
Not you.

A.Thorne-Miles

Your eyes are filled with the tales of the
oceans that could teach an entire
generation of flowers to bloom.
Go and blossom my love,
The world is waiting for you.

A.Thorne-Miles

It will never make it okay,
 being loved the right way
but the pain will ease with time.
The memories will become a haze
you will smile even on rainy days,
some days you will have to create your
own sunshine but that is okay. You'll get
through this. I promise.

A.Thorne-Miles

You need rain to create rainbows,
cry those tears
 there are colours in them
even the human eye can't see.
There are better days to come.
Love doesn't make you cry
 for the wrong reasons.

A.Thorne-Miles

Some days i'm afraid to go outside
 because of all the abuse
 but let me tell you something,
you get one life.

Whatever makes you feel alive again
 do it.
You are brave,
courageous
 and you are strong
never let somebody so small minded
intimidate you.

A.Thorne-Miles

Your abuser has not won.
The tortoise
 will always beat the hare.
Don't you dare
get caught up in your abusers
trap of
believing you did it to yourself.
You hold the trophies of millions
of women and men before you.
You are alive and that is something so
precious like you wouldn't understand
unless you've survived something so
cruel.

A.Thorne-Miles

You will eventually love yourself in the
way you were loved when mother earth
created you.
Just hang on in there.

A.Thorne-Miles

The storm can either pass
or you can dance in the rain
  knowing love is right under your nose.
It's you my darling,
you are the love you deserve.

A.Thorne-Miles

I promise it gets better.
You just have to love yourself first.
You are the first and last person
you come into this life with.
You're not alone,
you will always have you.

A.Thorne-Miles

You deserve the world, never forget it.

It is not your fault and it never will be.
You my dear are what makes the world
go round.
People like you, are the rarest of diamonds.

A.Thorne-Miles

Stay strong.
The tide will always pull back.

A.Thorne-Miles

You can find me on Instagram
@athornemilespoetry

Printed in Great Britain
by Amazon

83496011R00059